ABCs of Living a Good Life

26 Things I've Learned along the Way

DR. RUHANIYAH

authorHOUSE®

AuthorHouse™
1663 Liberty Drive
Bloomington, IN 47403
www.authorhouse.com
Phone: 1 (800) 839-8640

Published by AuthorHouse 04/20/2016

ISBN: 978-1-5246-0426-4 (sc)
ISBN: 978-1-5246-0425-7 (e)

Library of Congress Control Number: 2016906477

Print information available on the last page.

Any people depicted in stock imagery provided by Thinkstock are models,
and such images are being used for illustrative purposes only.
Certain stock imagery © Thinkstock.

This book is printed on acid-free paper.

Preface

When we look back on our life, we open a treasure chest of lessons learned. I've come to understand that the most trying times teach us the best lessons for personal growth.

It is my hope that you find something beneficial in this book. To this end, I have included pages for your own reflections on what each word means to you and in your life. There is also room for you to jot down any goals you may have regarding implementing the word into your life.

Acceptance

"Life is a series of natural and spontaneous changes. Don't resist them; that only creates sorrow. Let reality be reality. Let things flow naturally forward in whatever way they like." Lao Tzu

Acceptance comes with the appreciation of what is, without mourning what is not. Understanding that there are things that you cannot change, forget, or erase helps you to accept current and past realities. When you fail to accept what used to be or what currently is, you only invite suffering and heartache. The same can be said for the future: When you fail to accept the possibilities of what may be, you invite worry and insecurity.

These are things that I did not always know. Even now that I know, acceptance is a daily practice in my life. This is especially true now that I am the mother of a fiercely independent, free-spirited little girl. It is simple to try imposing my will on her even if it does not succeed. However, I have learned to just accept her in the moment. Instead of fighting to get her back to sleep when I just want thirty more minutes in bed, I remind myself to just accept the fact that she is wide awake and either wants to play, drink milk, or stand on the bed and look out the window counting trucks and buses that pass. This actually causes less stress on us both. While I may not exactly be happy with waking up with the birds, I allow us both to have peaceful mornings.

Many people have a hard time with acceptance; they feel that it is similar to giving up, giving in, surrendering, or like they are somehow saying that whatever was done to them is okay if they accept it. Acceptance is not about allowing yourself to be walked on, silencing yourself, or being a victim or martyr. It is about realizing what things you can change and which ones you cannot control. For the latter, acceptance is key. Either you accept things you cannot change or you let them make you miserable and eat you alive from the inside out.

People who have experienced abuse, trauma, and other injustices have an especially hard time with this concept. Of course certain things *should* not have happened, but the reality is that they did and they cannot be undone no matter how hard we fight to understand why something happened, why it happened to us, and so on.

Acceptance is not an excuse for apathy and inaction. Yes, you have to accept that the veteran on the street is homeless or that your child is failing class, but that does not mean that you do nothing; it does not mean that it is okay.

Other ways in which acceptance comes in handy is in relationships and even in traffic. Relationships run so much more smoothly when we fully accept our partner(s) without trying to change them by force or manipulation. Accepting them decreases our selfish expectations and emotional suffering. If you are stuck in traffic with a 20-minute drive taking 2 hours, you have the option to blow your horn, scream and yell, curse under your breath, or whatever you do; however, these things only intensify your experience of the situation by increasing your suffering. Next time you are stuck in traffic, try taking some deep breaths, turn on some relaxing music, listen to an audio book you never have time for, or do some chair dancing while you rock out to your favorite tunes.

How do you handle acceptance (including self-acceptance) in your life?

Reflection

Acceptance

Goals

1.

2.

3.

Beauty

"The most beautiful people we have known are those who have known defeat, known suffering, known struggle, known loss, and have found their way out of the depths." Elisabeth Kübler-Ross

Beauty is something that is seen, but also something that is experienced. It is seen in people's faces, natural landscapes, and in good deeds done with no expectations. It is both something that we may embody and something that may be displayed upon or even projected upon us. One of the greatest things about beauty, especially physical beauty, is that it is not unanimous. Nevertheless, there are standards of beauty in different societies that dictate how beauty should look and who possesses it.

While I know that I am beautiful in general and in my own ethnic cultural context, I know that my physical body is also seen as an assault on mainstream beauty standards within my national context. I am a dark-skinned, obese, knock-kneed, flat-footed African American woman with natural hair, thick lips, a flat face and button nose. For some, everything about my body is ugly; however, the beauty of it all is that I completely accept that reality and do not feel less beautiful because of it. This is especially true since I am most concerned with the beauty that lies within.

I can honestly look back at many years during my adolescence and early adulthood and admit that I was an ugly person inside. Although I possessed beautiful qualities like compassion and being of service to those in need, my anger and bitterness overshadowed that. I began to honor the beauty inside of me when I began to learn why I was so angry and bitter and decided that I was going to change. This is all to say that: 1) I value the type of beauty that will transcend death with me, and 2) those who are ugly inside have the potential to be beautiful.

Are there standards against which you measure your own beauty? Have you ever met (or were) an ugly person on the inside who allowed beauty to flow within with the right help and inspiration?

Reflection

Beauty

Goals

1.

2.

3.

Courage

"Life shrinks or expands in proportion to one's courage." Anaïs Nin

Courage is a charitable act. It is an act that gives; it gives energy and possibilities as it annihilates fear and trepidation. It naturally encourages. Just take a moment to think of the last time you saw a display of courage. How did it affect you?

In my life, I've shown both courage and cowardice. I've come to realize how our displays of courage encourage others, especially those with similar backgrounds or circumstances. They see us do things when we do not even realize anyone is watching us.. They see our courage and something inside of them either whispers or defiantly declares, "If she can do it, I can too!" Our acts of courage, no matter how small, pave the way for others.

There are many acts of courage that have paved the way for me in my life. In my most courageous moments I tell myself, 'The worst that can happen if I try this is that I fail. Big deal.' In my most apprehensive moments I tell myself, 'Those who have come before me did the same and more with much less. I owe it to myself and to them to at least try.' Some of the acts of courage that most commonly motivate me have to do with my ancestors, my parents, people in my family, and people with similar backgrounds and dreams.

I have often imagined what courage it must have taken Harriet Tubman to do what she did: She escaped slavery and repeatedly went back into the belly of the beast to guide other runaway slaves to freedom. I've also thought about other abolitionists who put themselves in harm's way by providing shelter and safe passage for runaway slaves, and people of my parents' generation who risked their freedom and safety fighting for civil rights.

What actions from people in your life have given you courage? Has anyone ever told you that they dared to try something because they modeled after you? If not already, in which areas of your life could you be more courageous?

Reflection

Courage

_____
_____
_____
_____
_____
_____
_____
_____
_____
_____
_____

Goals

1.

_____
_____
_____

2.

_____
_____
_____

3.

_____
_____

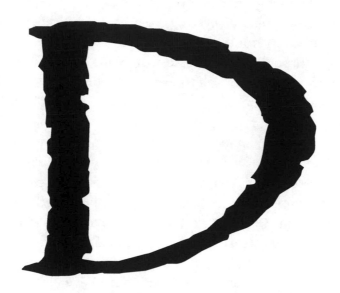

Dream

"Hold fast to dreams, for if dreams die
Life is a broken-winged bird, that cannot fly."

Langston Hughes

Dream is actually my daughter's middle name (but in Arabic). This is because she is my dream baby, my miracle baby girl. However, it is also because I want it to serve as a daily reminder to her in her life to hold fast to dreams that inspire and motivate her.

Many children grow up with only dreams to hold on to in order to keep hope alive in their lives...a dream of a better life in the future where love, safety, food, shelter, and freedom abound. Even many adults get through hard times on the wings of dreams. Dreams represent hope and life itself for many people. It helps many accept current realities while actively and inactively working to bring their dreams and aspirations into being.

Many of my childhood dreams have come true, but I still have dreams that I look forward to realizing. One of my childhood dreams was to be able to feel comfortable in my own "skin" as far as being authentically and organically me: nerdy, opinionated, clumsy, and hyper-emotional. One of the dreams I have had as an adult is to lead a 100% healthful lifestyle where I exercise and meditate regularly and only put healthful, wholesome, living energy food into my body. I've tried dozens of diets and have failed, but I have also changed my eating and activity for months at a time and lost up to 80 pounds just to gain it all back. I dream of the day that I become fit and healthy and remain that way for the rest of this life. This is not something that I expect to just happen overnight or without putting in hard work. I am fully aware that the realization of this dream depends on me, and the steps I'm taking are painstakingly slow but definitely progressive.

Some people don't believe in dreaming (or are simply afraid to dream), while others don't recognize that realizing their dream depends on actions that they take in their life. Dreams without action are just wishful thinking.

How do you work on manifesting your dreams? Are there dreams you had as a child that have come to fruition?

Reflection

Dreams

Goals

1.

2.

3.

Empathy

"All I ever wanted was to reach out and touch another human being not just with my hands but with my heart." Tahereh Mafi

Empathy is empowerment of and education about others in a deep connection of understanding one's experiences. It conjures up the concept of humanity's one-ness, and runs much deeper than compassion. With compassion, there is still the distinction of "you" and "me." It allows energetic and spiritual distance to remain between the compassionate one and the recipient of that compassion. Empathy, on the other hand, acts of a remover of that distance in such a way that "you" and "me" becomes "we." This is extremely important to be able to truly feel and understand with a sort of nomadic perspective.

I always remember being the person who wanted to reach out and touch others with my heart and soul. However, I was not sure how to do this, especially being an introvert. I was unable to do this for many of my younger years, but I can look back at some very trying experiences and see how I likely brought them into my life with the intention of growing my experiences in order to better understand others. For example, growing up I saw one of my close girlfriends and an adult family member in abusive relationships. I did not understand it, and I judged it harshly (especially the adult situation). I was raised by a strong mother and never saw my father raise a hand to her. I was brought up with the rhetoric of "never let a man put his hands on you." Nevertheless, I found myself in an abusive 4-year marriage with my first husband.

Although, I always fought back, my ex-husband was stronger. After one year of marriage, I knew the marriage was over and I had to end it, but it took three long years to figure out and execute an exit strategy that would not end up with me behind bars or dead. Until that experience, I was completely unable to empathize with women in abusive relationships. That experience caused me to question everything I knew about myself. It destroyed my facade, my egoic arrogance, and my previous paradigm. I look back at that experience and am thankful for how it cracked open my shell and allowed my soul to come out shining with such an openness and sensitivity to others' experiences.

I'd be remiss if I did not also mention how I've learned that being extremely sensitive to others' experiences also made me easily depleted of energy. It is easy to become depressed, anxious, and even irritated when you absorb everything around you. At times, being empathetic felt like a curse. Sometimes, I would even pray that it would go away. Thankfully, I've learned about energetic boundaries and self-care, which are still things I struggle to put into practice every day.

How do you define empathy? Would you describe yourself as empathetic? How do you think others would describe you?

Reflection

Empathy _____

_____
_____
_____
_____
_____
_____
_____
_____
_____
_____
_____
_____

Goals

1.

_____
_____
_____
_____

2.

_____
_____
_____
_____

3.

_____
_____
_____
_____

Faith

"Faith is the strength by which a shattered world
shall emerge into light." Helen Keller

Faith provides fortitude for the soul. Contrary to popular opinions, it does not necessarily have to be faith in a religious belief. Although, I follow a particular religious faith tradition, I define faith as "a belief and trust in and knowingness of the unseen and ineffable." It is powerful and a testament to the energy of belief, whether that belief is in God, Nature, healing, love, one's self, others, world peace, justice, etc. Faith is also tied to trust and hope, and is not exclusive.

I wake up every day with faith in the possibility of making it better than the day before. I sleep every night with faith that I will wake for another chance to right any wrongs done and get closer to becoming the person I want to be. I now allow myself to be vulnerable and live without secrets with faith that being open and honest will help others. I married my husband with faith in our commitment to another (ten years and counting!). We decided to have children with faith that we would be able to do so. We became parents with faith in our ability to do the very best for our daughter. I make plans for the future with faith that I will live to follow through with them.

During the two darkest times in my life, I have temporarily lost faith in everything, to the point that everything became nothing; I was nothing and was surrounded by nothingness. Faith in things getting better, that my feelings of hopelessness would subside, and hope that my resilience and buoyancy would propel me from the dark abyss are all I had.

How do you define faith? In what do you have faith? Was there ever a time when you lost your faith? If so, what did you do?

Reflection

Faith

Goals

1.

2.

3.

Gratitude

"Cultivate the habit of being grateful for every good thing that comes to you, and to give thanks continuously. And because all things have contributed to your advancement, you should include all things in your gratitude." Ralph Waldo Emerson

Gratitude is not just a feeling or words, it is an attitude and a practice.

Growing up, I had a really bad habit of focusing on and verbalizing the negative. All my life, my mother would remind me to be grateful for things and abilities I did have, especially considering the central nervous system disorder I was born with and just how differently I could have really been. She would always say, "Count your blessings, and thank God!" There is no doubt that her constant reminders changed me from an excessively complaining, negative child to a pretty positive and optimistic adult. (Thanks, mommy!)

Over the years, there were many times in my life when I did not believe that I had anything for which to be grateful. In those times, I'd hear my mother's voice in my head saying, "Well, then be grateful for your sight, ability to think, the air you breathe, your feet and hands!" Over time, I began to really embrace gratitude as a daily practice. I noticed how it changed my perspective throughout the day. Although I do not keep a gratitude journal, I am in the habit of ending each of my days lying in my bed and going down a mental list of things for which I am grateful. This lists includes general things that are constants in my life, but also particular things that may have happened during the day.

Along the way, I've learned that gratitude is not just for things bestowed upon us, but also for the things withheld from us. With an attitude of gratitude, there is little to no room for emptiness, envy, jealousy, or insufficiency. Gratitude is not only looking at the glass half full, but being thankful for the water, the glass, and the gift of the senses that allow you to perceive the water in the glass at all.

How do you make gratitude a daily practice? If you don't yet, how can you? Was there a time during which you were ungrateful? If so, what changed you? If you've always had an attitude of gratitude, to what do you attribute it?

Reflection

Gratitude

Goals

1.

2.

3.

Health

"A further sign of health is that we don't become undone by fear and trembling, but we take it as a message that it's time to stop struggling and look directly at what's threatening us." Pema Chödrön

Health is considered to be our wealth by many, and this is one lesson I learned later in life than many. It is one of those things that we often don't appreciate or even pay attention to until it's gone. It is the optimum state of being.

Often, discussions of health only include physical health, to the point that schools promote physical health through offering physical education time (much less common nowadays). While it is great that children's education involves physical health, there are many facets of health that are ignored: mental, emotional, financial, and spiritual health. I have found that society is obsessed with physical health using mainstream "beauty" and thinness as markers of health. In my household, my parents were concerned about my physical health, but they also paid heavy attention to my spiritual health. Emotional and financial health were not things I even thought about as a young person. Having my emotional health in serious jeopardy caused me to really start seeing it as my wealth. I realized that when I was not well inside, nothing was right. It was not the actual things, but more of my perception of things that was so skewed.

Having a serious mind-body disconnect, I am just recently realizing how important physical health really is, especially since becoming a mother and seeing how my lifestyle will inform my daughter's. This realization caused me to start thinking about terms I call "intra-health" and "inter-health," with the former being the state within an individual and the latter focusing on the state in relationships (in my example, this was the mother-daughter relationship). I take very seriously the fact that my daughter's intra-health is heavily dependent upon my intra-health.

What do you consider to be health? Are you healthy? In which ways? If not, what do you need to do to achieve health in those areas?

Reflection

Health

Goals

1.

2.

3.

Imagination

"Imagination does not become great until human beings, given the courage and the strength, use it to create." Maria Montessori

Imagination is that magical thing that we often lose as we grow into adulthood. It is a gift. It is something that allows us to traverse the world in 7 seconds or even travel back to far gone eras for minutes at a time if we wish. It also has the ability to breathe life into us and open us up to endless possibilities. It is the cradle of innovation. Imagination can also usher in healing, provide inspiration and hope.

My imagination fuels me; it is where my creativity resides. It allows me to be weightless and without the boundaries of reality and reason. In my imagination, I get to do the undoable and think the unthinkable. It is the master behind my vision boards and that mischievous smile and blank stare some say I get when I day dream.

Imagination is like visualization in that it can become a purposeful daily practice to promote wellbeing and healing. As someone who has been overweight and obese practically my entire life, I have no idea what it's like to have a fit and slender body. However, finally being able to imagine myself that way helps me to have faith that it is in reach. We imagine goals before we achieve them; we must imagine them in order to be able to define them and devise an action plan to get us there. When we imagine things a certain way, we bring them closer to reality.

While I engage in wild imagination often, I also practice self-guided imagination. Both have their place and serve their purpose in my life. For example, each time I had a miscarriage, I imagined our child's faces and their energy still being with me beyond the flesh. I imagined each child wiping my tears (even the ones I could not bear to shed) and whispering with such sweetness, "Don't worry. Another one is coming, mommy." In those long moments of disappointment, despair, emptiness, and even anger; imagination poured healing, holy water over my soul and into my wounds.

Do you pay attention to your imagination? Is it important to you? Where does it take you?

Reflection

Imagination _____

_____

_____

_____

_____

_____

_____

_____

_____

_____

_____

Goals

1.

_____

_____

_____

2.

_____

_____

_____

3.

_____

_____

_____

_____

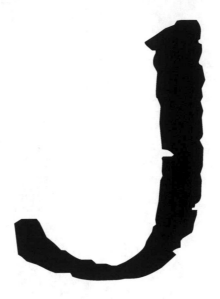

Justice

"Justice will not be served until those who are unaffected
are as outraged as those who are." Benjamin Franklin

Justice is one of those tricky concepts that has many faces, especially for survivors of violence. For many, justice is restorative where they are willing to engage in a dialogue with the perpetrator, community, and other stakeholders to attempt to repair the harm that has been done to them. For others, justice is poetic. It comes in the form of retribution and punishment whether it involves incarceration, physical harm or illness, or death by homicide or suicide. Yet others feel that there is no such thing as justice any way you look at it. They feel that there is nothing that can ever be said or done to erase or minimize the effects of violence. No form of justice is necessarily better than another.

It is all about healing. If justice does not provide some sort of healing, it is not justice in my eyes. Many survivors of violence spend years and decades searching for peace and healing through justice. Some of us will find it, while others may not. My justice-seeking journey has been a long and arduous one. At that point when I realized that certain forms of outward justice were no longer viable options, I embarked on a sort of archeological dig deep within myself to find out exactly what I was searching for when I kept saying that I wanted justice. Repeatedly, the answer was that I wanted to find healing, gaping wound-by-gaping wound, scar-by-scar, cell-by-cell, memory-by-memory. This is when I started focusing all the mental and emotional energy that I wasted on concepts of outward justice and turned it inward.

I decided to create my own justice instead of asking others for it or sitting around waiting for it, and I am not finished yet. Justice is a journey for me. I can never get my life back from before certain injustices were done, but I can and do reclaim my life for myself right now; I do it every day. It is a constantly renewing commitment. Living my best life, being my best me, speaking my truth, and defining myself for myself ushers justice my way. I have come to see that finding peace and healing does not have to depend on whether the perpetrators of violence against me are repentant, in physical pain, behind bars, or under the ground in a grave. My journey has taught me that I am powerful enough that my justice is whatever I decide it is, and the same is true for you.

Dr. Ruhaniyah

How do you define justice? Are there certain areas in which you have achieved justice? In which areas do you still feel that justice has not been served? What can you do about this? If there are ways in which you treated someone unjustly (even yourself), what can you do to make it right?

Reflection

Justice

Goals

1.

2.

3.

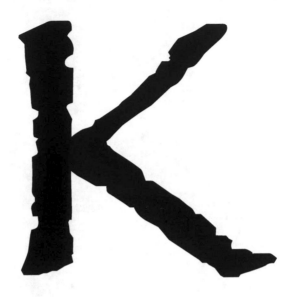

Knowledge

"When you know a thing, to hold that you know it,
and when you do not know a thing, to allow that you
do not know it - this is knowledge." Confucius

Knowledge is not only gained in the pages of schoolbooks; it is gained from looking deep within ourselves and into our surroundings. It is true that with the more knowledge we gain, the more capable we become of seeing just how much there is that we do not know. It is one of those perpetual journeys where, hopefully, we never quite arrive at our destination.

Contemplating knowledge always makes me think of two of my father's sayings, "The universe is a university" and "the world is a one-room classroom" (thanks, daddy!). We may all be at different stages of learning, but we are all on a journey for knowledge. For an introvert or recluse, that may be a deep knowledge of self. For the extrovert or sociable person, that may be the deep knowledge of human behavior and social cues.

For me, I was an introvert who thrived academically. I gained so much academic knowledge, skipped grades, and won numerous scholastic competitions. However, I lacked "common sense" and social knowledge. I remember feeling so powerful as a student, but disempowered (and withdrawn because of it) in social situations. It took some very hard lessons in the School of Hard Knocks to teach me that knowledge extended far beyond the classroom. Having always been one of the smartest students, I did not know how to navigate the struggle in the classroom of life. This is when knowing came in for me. Even without street knowledge or common sense, I had a deep sense of knowing that I would learn the lessons I needed to learn no matter how tough it got.

There is another form of knowledge that I often refer to as "knowing" or "knowingness." Knowingness is that knowledge that is innate; we just have it. For example, the baby knows to cry, our lungs know to breathe, our eyes know to blink. For me, I just knew that one day I would know. While, I had rational knowledge, I began to actively seek emotional knowledge since I knew that I was thoroughly lacking in that area. The greatest part of the knowledge journey is knowing that I still don't know it all. It is actually exciting to wonder about what new things I will learn each day.

How has your knowledge journey shaped your life? Are there particular areas in which you feel extremely knowledgeable? How about the areas in which you have the least amount of knowledge?

Reflection

Knowledge

Goals

1.

2.

3.

Loyalty

"Achievement of your happiness is the only moral purpose of your life, and that happiness, not pain or mindless self-indulgence, is the proof of your moral integrity, since it is the proof and the result of your loyalty to the achievement of your values." Ayn Rand

Loyalty can be to people, principles, and your word. Many of us are fortunate enough to learn its meaning very young, though we may not learn its value until later.

When we grow up feeling strongly supported by our family, we develop a healthy sense of loyalty and allegiance to the family unit. We know we can count on family members to fulfill certain needs. When we grow up without such support (and many times even with it), we may obsessively look for loyalty elsewhere-street gangs, organized crime syndicates, religions, cults, the military, the police force, political parties, monogamous relationships, and elsewhere. Or, the opposite can occur: we may persistently avoid situations where loyalty is required.

In my 20s, I really grappled with the idea of loyalty; it kept me up at night and often held an invisible hand over my mouth. Ultimately, I had to reshape my thinking and learn that loyalty is something that is earned and deserved; it's not always a healthy thing; and, most importantly, I deserve to be the recipient of my own loyalty. Once I learned these things, I had to make the extremely difficult decision to choose loyalty to self over loyalty to the family unit.

While there are many ways and reasons to be more loyal to oneself over one's own family, my decision was necessary for my healing after years of dealing with the debilitating aftereffects of incestuous sexual abuse. I thought that exposing this extended family member who often came to live with us was, somehow, wrong, shameful and detrimental to the family's happiness, wellbeing and cohesion. I used to lie awake at night filled with grief and anger wondering, 'What about MY happiness, wellbeing, and the integration of my mind and body?!' This anguish was not just regarding loyalty to my blood family, but also loyalty to my husband at that time.

Childhood sexual abuse is a wide gateway to future intimate partner violence (IPV). Needless to say, loyalty to my first husband nearly cost me my life...twice. From the outside looking in, the abused partner may look like a stupid person who must love being beaten. However, the reality is extremely complicated and involves issues of loyalty. In my case, in the beginning of the abuse, I was trying to be what I thought was a loyal wife: helping him to change his ways, being patient, nonjudgmental, not being quick to leave or divorce him, not telling others about his problems or what was happening behind closed doors.

So, while loyalty can be a wonderful thing in families and romantic relationships, as well as among friends and comrades; it can also silence and damage. Life has taught me that in its heart of hearts, loyalty is a comforting blessing. Loyalty is what we make it; so, make it safe and beautiful.

How have your life experiences shaped you to define loyalty? Has there been a time when you had to choose loyalty to yourself over another person or group of people? How did this make you feel? Did something in you change as a result?

Reflection

Loyalty

Goals

1.

2.

3.

Mindfulness

"The present moment is filled with joy and happiness.
If you are attentive, you will see it." Thich Nhất Hanh

Mindfulness is a practice and a state of being actively open to and engaged with the present moment. It is living in the present moment's experience without judgment nor expectation. It is a state in which the broken record playing in our head ceases and we are one with our inner experience. Many people seek a state of mindfulness through using legal and illegal drugs. It is definitely a shortcut to what can be accomplished through prayer, meditation, yoga, sitting in Nature, listening to a hymn or favorite song, dancing, exercise or deep breathing.

Mindfulness is something that I would have loved to have learned as a child. It's one of those skills that young people should be taught along with financial literacy and responsibility, critical thinking, and other important life subjects. I grasped the concept later in life though I had experienced it very intensely and repeatedly during a summer stay on the Caribbean coast of Panama when I was 17. After completing my research project on Afro-Panamanians, I had absolutely nothing to do. By default, I just began being in each moment and soaking in all the beauty around me. Even with experience as a teen, mindfulness as an adult was a foreign concept to me. This was especially true because what happened in Panama was a gift from the Universe, while trying to conjure up and be deliberate about mindfulness, at a time when I desperately needed it, was escaping me.

As a very emotional person who lives with PTSD (posttraumatic stress disorder), bipolar depression and anxiety; practicing mindfulness has helped me come back to my center during the flood of negative emotions, flashbacks, and night terrors. It used to be extremely difficult to experience the present moment when I spent much of my childhood mentally and emotionally escaping from physical, sexual, and verbal abuse. It took a long time to be successful at my mindfulness attempts. The incessant voice of my inner critic was so hard to shut up. When it finally did give me respite, the worry-wart showed up with all its what-ifs and whys. Then, my internal accuser's assistant with all its should haves, would haves, could haves appeared followed by the saboteur with her whispers of things like, "You'll only last with this whole mindfulness business for a little while" and "Just forget it; it's not working anyway!" I'm so glad I stuck with it long enough to see that I could achieve it over and over again. You can too!

If you are already a mindfulness master, how did you get started? What obstacles did you need to overcome? If you would like to start on your mindfulness journey, list some steps you think will be helpful or even some obstacles and creative ways to overcome them.

Dr. Ruhaniyah

Reflection

Mindfulness

Goals

1.

2.

3.

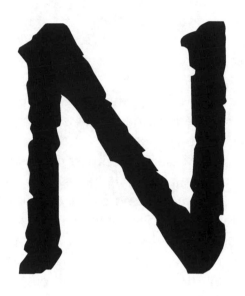

Nurture

"Be the one who nurtures and builds. Be the one
who has an understanding and a forgiving heart,
one who looks for the best in people. Leave people
better than you found them." Marvin J. Ashton

Nurture is part of our nature; it is instinctual. Parents, older siblings, mentors and teachers nurture and mold young minds. Nevertheless, everyone has the power to nurture others and themselves with a loving touch, a kind word, or a helpful action. We can all do something to encourage the growth and healthy development of others (and ourselves).

It is easy to focus on the negative, to critique, and to judge. For many people, this is all they know how to do. It does not come naturally to them to say a kind word of encouragement. It may not even be easy for them to accept the kind words of others. Even for those who did not experience nurture, it is a divine skill that can be learned and used to heal the self and others. It can start with you, and the blessings that you bring to others can be boundless.

I've come to see nurturing as having a nutritional value to it. Positive talk, affirmations, and praise can be as important as eating our vegetables and drinking enough water. Without certain nutrients, our bodies wither and die. The same is true for our souls and psyche. Also, the offering and receiving of nurture can be very different. I receive nurture in many ways, although my favorites and easiest for me to receive are: affirming words and physical touch from trusted loved ones.

Growing up as an exceptional student in my school environments, I was often praised for academic achievements but ridiculed for social behaviors. The part of me that receives healthy physical touch as nurture did not thrive as a child. My family culture did not include displays of emotion (anger was partially acceptable) or affection. I may have seen my parents hold hands and kiss once. (Interestingly, my parents do show more affectionate now.) While my parents nurtured us in various ways, physical touch was not one. When I finally had my first romantic relationship at 19 years old, I would become so irritated when he would hold my hand. I would always think, 'What the heck is he holding my hand for, as if I cannot see? I know where we're going!' It took several dates with him for me to realize that this was one way in which people showed affection. It made me realize how much I was stuck in emotional infancy. So, I began the journey of allowing touch, touching others, liking touch, and then needing it. I realized that there was a large void, an underdeveloped part of me, and I began touching myself with nurture in the form of seemingly silly self-hugs and caresses; I'd even hold my own hand when falling asleep.

Are you a nurturing person? In what ways could you use more nurturing?

Reflection

Nurture

Goals

1.

2.

3.

Overcome

"Many people pray to be kept out of unexpected problems.
Some people pray to be able to confront
and overcome them." Toba Beta

Overcome is one of those words that if it had a body, it would stand tall with pride in its accomplishments, yet would have signs of wear and tear from its arduous journeys.

Overcoming obstacles, whether physical or mental, imposed or self-imposed, real or imagined; requires resilience, buoyancy, and the desire and belief that things can get better and that you play the key role in making them better.

There are those who have overcome great physical obstacles, those who doctors said would never wake from a coma, walk again after paralysis, or even something as simple (yet complex) as the single sperm, among millions, that overcomes grueling physical obstacles in a foreign environment to penetrate the ovum.

I've learned that overcoming is not just a physical action or feat; it is a state of mind. In this state of mind, self-pity cannot survive and victimhood cannot thrive. It requires that the one to overcome believes and behaves as if s/he is bigger and better than any obstacle in the way. That obstacle may be flawed thinking, skewed perspective, a traumatic event, mental illness, physical illness, financial poverty and more.

The idea of overcoming challenges always makes me think of one of my father's mantras, "Success, anyhow!" In spite of your circumstances now or in the past, you have the capacity and must have the will to overcome. The process of overcoming does not have to be done alone; it is best done with the support and encouragement of others who have traveled on similar paths and have triumphed.

What obstacles have you overcome in your life? What are any current obstacles you face? How can you overcome them? Will you enlist anyone's assistance?

Reflection

Overcome _____

_____

_____

_____

_____

_____

_____

_____

_____

_____

_____

_____

Goals

1.

_____

_____

_____

_____

2.

_____

_____

_____

3.

_____

_____

_____

_____

Peace

"Peace begins with a smile." Mother Theresa

Peace has an outer and an inner reality. It can be displayed in peaceful, non-violent communication or activism, or in many other ways. It is synonymous to harmony, and some even refer to it as the absence of war.

It is difficult to think of those people in the world, especially children, who have never experienced peace in their lives. Peace is something that is spoken of as if it is the universal norm, the default, a human rights reality; but the reality is that it is a privilege and luxury that far too many have never and will probably never enjoy. Some may be lucky enough to enjoy peace intermittently in their lifetime. To imagine that adults and children cross dangerous land and water borders, traverse countries and continents in search of peace, a peace that I enjoy every day, nearly takes my breath away. Then, what of those who live in places where peace is abundant except in their own homes?

Peace in the home life is often overlooked but is crucial for those lucky enough to have a home and loved ones with whom to share it. While my country, city, and neighborhood were all peaceful, my home was once a war zone.

There were many days and nights when I finished a day of teaching and parked my car in a grocery store parking lot to sleep or just sit in safe solitude instead of going straight home to the chaos that awaited me with my first husband. After long days often battling my way through five and six periods of high school students, I just could not imagine going straight into the war zone I called "home." I would stay out as long as I could each day because that meant that there were fewer hours spent at home enduring chaos and violence. I was an adult who only found some sort of peace when alone in the confines of my vehicle, but that peace was really only physical. Even after I divorced and found physical safety and peace once again, I still did not have peace in my mind. There was still the battlefield in my mind with which I had to deal. I don't know what it must be like for children who directly and indirectly experience violence in the home on a daily basis. The one place where we should all be safe and experience peace is in the home.

Did you have a peaceful childhood? How? If not, Why not? Do you have peace in your life now? If you do, how did you obtain it? If not, what is in your control to help you obtain it?

Reflection

Peace

Goals

1.

2.

3.

Quietude

"Only let the moving waters calm down, and the sun and moon will be reflected on the surface of your being." Rumi

Quietude is a sense of inner peace, stillness, and calm. We usually experience this when we sleep. Before cell phones became appendages, people often used the bathroom as a place of quietude. As a mother of a toddler, I often use the bathroom as a refuge for peace and quiet (it only works when my daughter is not in the bathroom with me or banging on the door trying to come in). Many people enjoy quietude when they pray or meditate. I experience a great level of this when I am at the ocean listening to the waves or swimming weightlessly in a pool of water.

There are many people who run from quietude. There are various reasons why, but I used to run from it when I was a young child because my thoughts would become so loud whenever I sat in solitude. I would wonder about the universe, my life in the womb, my purpose in life, why I did not see heaven on my first airplane flight across the country, what will happen to me after I die, the concept of infinity, and things like this. I would find myself going down the rabbit hole and working myself into a state of anxiety because I only had questions at that time with no answers. I distinctly remember the first time I ever questioned my fear of quietude. I was chattering when my father said, "You know that you don't have to talk when you really don't have anything to say, right? Think of it like there is limited oxygen and use your voice wisely by not wasting the oxygen that someone else could be using." That was a pivotal moment in my development. I became more discerning in my use of language and my motives for talking. If it was just to say something so that my thoughts would shut up, I would stay quiet and sit with my thoughts.

At about 12 years old I learned to really love and revel in solitude and quietude. I began to write poetry and really reflect on Nature and the order of things. I also started arriving at answers to my many questions. I felt great kinship when I first learned about Transcendentalism when I was 13. It let me see that I was not crazy for the thoughts I had been having since I was much younger, and that if I was crazy, at least I was not alone for people long before me had similar thoughts about the world and the order of things.

How do you make time to experience quietude in your life? What are some of the benefits of stillness?

Reflection

Quietude

_____

Goals

1.

2.

3.

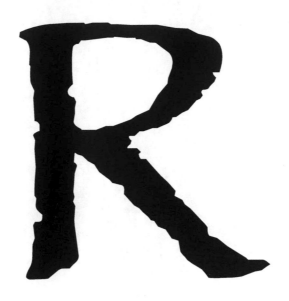

Respect

"Let today be the day...You look for the good in everyone you meet and respect their journey."

Steve Maraboli

Respect is something that many say must be earned. Not only must it be earned in many circumstances, it must also be maintained. Nevertheless, I do not consider this to be true for all. For example, I believe that babies' and children's bodies and minds deserve respect automatically and without question. I also subscribe to certain societal norms like that the elderly automatically deserve a level of generational respect, as well as laws and figures of authority.

We often focus on being respected rather than being respectable. I remember growing up I always demanded to be respected, especially in school by authority figures. Yet, most times I did not behave respectably and hardly ever respectfully toward others. Looking back, I understand why it was so difficult for most of my teachers to offer me the respect I so desired. I believe that I always deserved respect as a human being and child, and even as a very bright student; but I did not earn respect with my terrible behavior and disrespectful outbursts. Respecting others is just as important as respecting ourselves.

I've thought a lot about respecting boundaries. Can you truly respect someone if you refuse to respect their boundaries? I have especially wondered about this in relationships (friends, lovers, siblings, parents, children, etc.) Although we may love and care for someone, we do not really respect them if we do not know and respect their boundaries.

What about respecting children? Do they have to earn your respect or is it automatically given?

What about respect for Nature? Does Nature have to earn your respect or is it simply given?

Reflection

R espect

Goals

1.

2.

3.

Service

"I slept and dreamt that life was joy. I awoke
and saw that life was service.

I acted and behold, service was joy." Rabindranath Tagore

Service is a sacred form of worship or acknowledgement of one-ness. I used to be extremely selfish as a child and young adult. It was not until I started looking at service as: 1) *seva* (from Hindu and Sikh traditions) and 2) *sadaqah* (a form of charity from my own religion) that gives to the giver and the receiver. I began to see how serving others did not take away from me. I found myself more joyful and more fulfilled the more I engaged in authentic, self-authored acts of service. One of the only memories I have of being engaged in service and truly being in the moment and enjoying it was when I volunteered with the Special Olympics when I was a teenager. I felt so happy and infused with joy being surrounded by all the smiles and dedication. Even though I just ran alongside competitors to cheer them on or gave them water or hugs when they wanted them, I felt like there was nowhere else on earth I would rather be; I felt truly connected and plugged in.

Over the years, I have volunteered in many ways, but I have learned that service is not always a conscious decision to go out to a location and volunteer. I started being of service in much more natural ways like opening doors for people, translating if I saw someone struggling to be understood or understand, being a better listener, and things like this. Sometimes my service was like an offering to God to say, "Thank You" for bestowing certain gifts and talents upon me. Other times, my service was to honor the people I was serving. Now, it is part of my daily devotional practice and acknowledgement of one-ness. What I have learned on my journey from self-centered and action-centered service to seeing service as a state of mind and heart is best summed up by something I read long ago by Sri Sri Ravi Shankar:

Service is the expression of love. Serve in whatever possible manner you can. Ask yourself, "How can I be useful to people around me, and to the whole world?" Then your heart starts blossoming and a completely new level begins. Otherwise we're always thinking, "What about me, what about me?" It's nothing! Ask, "How can I be useful, how can I give to the world?

In which ways do you make yourself of service to others? How do you feel when you give freely to others? Are there ways in which you make yourself of service to yourself? How might you integrate service more naturally into your everyday life?

Reflection

Service

_____

_____

_____

_____

_____

_____

_____

_____

_____

_____

_____

_____

_____

Goals

1.

_____

_____

_____

_____

2.

_____

_____

_____

_____

3.

_____

_____

_____

_____

Tradition

"Tradition is a guide and not a jailer."
W. Somerset Maugham

   Traditions are beliefs or practices that are orally and experientially transmitted from one generation to the next. Traditions can be religious, national, familial, societal, ethnic, and they can be good or bad depending on who is evaluating them.

   I grew up with very few traditions in my home. We did not really celebrate any religious or national holidays. However, I do remember a few traditions that I cherish. My paternal and maternal families are different religions, and the one holiday we all did share together many years is Thanksgiving, as it is not overtly religious. The foods we ate were also traditional (ethnically) during Thanksgiving dinner. We had baked macaroni and cheese, greens, black-eyed peas, corn bread, sock-it-to-me cake, and bean pie. Another tradition (familial) that is close to my heart is having homemade ice cream cake on our birthdays. My mom would bake a Bundt cake, slice it horizontally, add layers of different flavored sherbet, and cover the cake in rainbow sherbet and freeze it. It was so delicious! I definitely plan to continue this with my daughter when she is older. When I was a teenager, we celebrated Kwanzaa. That was very educational and empowering; it sparked my love for the Swahili language. Two other traditions I cherish and plan to continue are: 1) RVing every August until we had visited all 48 contiguous states and 2) my mom taking us to Rosarito, Mexico every Labor Day weekend before school started.

   When I was a child, I resented not celebrating religious or national holidays. We never had firecrackers for July 4th, no presents on Christmas, no Easter egg hunts or Halloween costumes. However, I later understood my parents reasoning that by not spending money on those things allowed them to save for us all to have different experiences (like travel). I plan to keep with this tradition with a few minor tweaks for our daughter, especially as it relates to our religious traditions.

   I had always thought that traditions were a good thing until I grew older and wiser. I lived life for about 15 years dressing very traditionally for my religion and following conservative traditions that did not agree with my heart. I had to learn that it was ok to still follow a faith tradition even if I did not subscribe to or practice certain things with which my mind and soul disagreed. For example, traditionally, I should be against anything other than monogamous heterosexuality and many other things, but I see love as being so grand as to be without bounds and limits. However, thanks to my upbringing and coming full circle with myself, I am secure knowing that I do not have to mold myself to fit into certain traditions, I open my arms to those traditions that agree with my consciousness and conscience.

Do you have traditions that you follow? What are they? What are your beliefs about the merits of tradition? Are there certain traditions that you refuse to follow or pass on?

Reflection

Tradition

Goals

1.

2.

3.

Understanding

"I think that hate is a feeling that can only exist
where there is no understanding."

Tennessee Williams

Understanding lends itself to empathy and peace, as well as wisdom and enlightenment. There are two sides to understanding: 1) understanding of oneself and 2) understanding of others.

Understanding ourselves is the greatest gift we can grant ourselves and the world. We must understand our heart, mind, soul, and ego. This all helps us understand our reality, our perceptions, our intentions, and our actions and interactions. Childhood trauma caused me to search for understanding very young. I needed to know why I was on earth if I was silently suffering so much. I often thought it would have been better to be unborn than endure such sexual abuse and personal violation. My spirit and mind came to an understanding that although my body had to endure certain things with emotional aftereffects, they would work extremely hard together to shield me from this harm by disassociating from my body and allowing my brain to pretend these horrible things were happening to someone else. After many years of amnesia regarding the abuse, my spirit and mind deemed me ready to remember it.

Understanding myself has also allowed me to practice a lot of compassionate toward myself and my inner child. They say that a part of the traumatized child stays the age at which the trauma occurs. For years, I ignored and then shunned my inner child; that is, until I came into understanding. As an educator, I found understanding myself to be crucial. It allowed me to know my starting point-of-reference from which I teach, and purposefully close the gap between that and my students' learning.

Understanding others and their positionality (positioned reality) in this world allows for compassion and empathy. Many confuse acceptance with understanding. It is possible to accept someone without understanding them and to understand them without accepting them. I first realized this distinction in a major way when one of my brothers "came out" as gay; he was 19 and I was 16. I fully accepted him, but I did not understand him for many years. The same can be said for me. Aside from this same brother, no one in my family understands me; however, they all accept me.

Dr. Ruhaniyah

Is there a time when you remember finally understanding yourself? Have you ever misunderstood someone and it caused them or you harm? How do you feel about understanding versus acceptance? Are there ways in which you can be more self-understanding and understanding of others?

Reflection

Understanding _____

_____

_____

_____

_____

_____

_____

_____

_____

_____

_____

_____

_____

_____

Goals

1.

_____

_____

_____

_____

2.

_____

_____

_____

_____

3.

_____

_____

_____

_____

Vulnerability

"I understand now that the vulnerability I've always felt is the greatest strength a person can have." Elisabeth Shue

Vulnerability is one way to be victorious in your life. Most are afraid to be vulnerable whether it is at work, among friends, with a lover, etc. Vulnerability is like a layer of skin that may remain impermeable to things like water but are permeable to other things. It is not about walking around skinless and allowing every touch and movement of the wind to cause pain. It is more about being semi-permeable allowing the smaller molecular structures of grace and love to flow in through the cracks.

As a young person, I survived by becoming as invulnerable as I could. I was even called "Ice Queen" and "Ice Bitch" by people. I acted as though I had armor around everything but my brain. My brain was always so open to learning, but my body refused to be touched with hugs or hand-holding and my heart was a fortress. While I had crushes, I never truly dated. I first allowed myself to be vulnerable when I was 19 and met a man. Feeling such love broke my barriers wide open. Unfortunately, this man (my first husband) turned out to be abusive. Nevertheless, I am able to see the good that the universe allowed him to bring into my emotional development.

Throughout my life, vulnerability has caused great pain and wonderfully pleasurable experiences. It comes with the territory of opening oneself up that some bad will come with the good. Being vulnerable means some will take advantage of our kindness or mistake our purposeful vulnerability with weakness or passivity. I have found that love requires vulnerability. Loving someone is a risk we take in being vulnerable to either the greatest love ever, the worst, or somewhere in between.

People often think that being vulnerable means being weak. I used to think the same. Although it can involve being weak, it does not have to...does it? Do you allow yourself to be vulnerable? If yes, in which ways? If no, why not?

Reflection

Vulnerability

Goals

1.

2.

3.

Wealth

"Wealth consists not in having great possessions, but in having few wants."

Epictetus

Wealth is in your health and wellness, as well as in your wisdom and relationships. Some of the wealthiest people I have ever known are those who are financially poor. Their wealth is in their relationships and wellness. I have also witnessed great wealth in older people who are full of wisdom and knowledge.

Having had periods of poor physical, mental, and spiritual health; I learned that the health and wellness of all of those parts of me are large portions of my non-monetary wealth. With my asthma, it was so easy to take for granted the wealth my breath brings me when all was well. However, when my asthma flared and I had trouble breathing and completing daily tasks, I realized what a gift air and properly functioning lungs were. Having a central nervous system disorder, various parts of my body are affected. I have fewer teeth than average and most are still my baby teeth. This causes issues with my dental health that, thankfully, I have the funds to correct as they occur. Having teeth problems has made me so much more thankful for even having teeth at all. My mental illnesses have affected my health and wealth at different times in my life. When my mental state has been poor, I isolated myself from those I needed most. This further decreased my overall wealth because I no longer had rich relationships to lean on or other people's wisdom from which to benefit.

With my heath issues, I also began to see that money was wealth, but only in so far as what it could buy me. It could buy me better medicines, better doctors, better treatments that may lead to my sense of health and wellness. So, I don't say that wealth is health and wellness as a way to reject the power of monetary wealth.

In which ways do you consider yourself wealthy? It could be your talents and gifts, the people you know, your academic qualifications, etc. In which ways do you consider yourself poor? What can you do to increase your wealth in those areas?

Reflection

Wealth

Goals

1.

2.

3.

Xenia

"Hospitality [Xenia] means primarily the creation of free space where the stranger can enter and become a friend instead of an enemy." Henri J.M. Nouwen

Xenia is a fancy way of saying "hospitality." Xenial is a way of being hospitable. Not only must we learn how to be xenial to ourselves, but also to others. Everyone is like a traveler in this world needing rest stops here and there to replenish their soul, needing a place to lay their head, or a simple and safe encounter. It is easier to say than to do, but we should try to always be xenial as everyone is fighting their own inward and/or outward battle in this often not-so-kind-world.

I have come to see that being xenial is much harder when we are the recipient. We are often very harsh with ourselves, and may even berate ourselves with our inner talk. I have often said that the worst bully is the one inside our own mind that torments us on a daily basis until we learn to tame it. I used to be a perfectionist and severely self-critical. I would think things about myself and say them to myself when I would never even dream of saying such things even to an enemy. For our entire lifetime we are stuck with our self, so we might as well be xenial to it.

As far as how we treat other people who come into our lives for just moments or for years, being xenial can come easy or be a challenge. I can look back and remember times in which I behaved terribly toward people. The worst memory is when I removed a really good friend in my life simply because my ex-husband told me to do it. She was so kind and was my best friend. She knew me in ways no one else did. She even came to live with us for a while. Yet, I suddenly kicked her out and refused to talk to her. Now, almost 20 years later, I still think about how poorly I behaved toward her. However, over the last three years, I was finally able to forgive myself without knowing whether she has or not.

I have also learned that being xenial does not mean that I have to be a doormat or than I can never say, "No." My boundaries are still important.

Do you consider yourself to be hospitable? In which ways do you practice hospitality? Are there areas in which you think you could improve?

Reflection

Xenia

Goals

1.

2.

3.

Yes

"There are an infinite number of reasons to say no.
Instead, try to focus on one good reason to say yes." Jarod Kintz

Yes is something you can begin to say more when it comes to trying new things and being adventurous. However, reserving your right to say no to certain things is extremely important to remember.

I used to consider myself a cautious person, but I found myself often saying no to possibly fun opportunities. I still remember the first big time I said, "Yes!" to myself. One night, after six years of sexual abuse, I finally stood up to my abuser. I don't know why that night was different; I just know that I was tired of my body not being my own. In that moment of rebellion, I symbolically said "YES!" to myself, to my safety, to my body, and to my life. Prior to that, I used to pretend that my body was not my own, so reclaiming my body as mine was potentially dangerous and completely revolutionary for me. Yet, it was a chance I had to take on myself.

The second time I said yes to myself was when I decided that I wanted to study in Barcelona, Spain by myself. I had never been away from home for longer than a week or traveled on my own before, but my soul called me to do something extraordinary. Normally, I would have said no to myself and dismissed the thought. However, the thought of studying abroad alone became an obsession. I was still a minor so I researched independent educational programs that would allow me to stay in a host family. While living abroad, I continued to say yes to adventure and once-in-a-lifetime experiences.

Another important time where I had to say yes to myself was when I chose me over my ex-husband. I had to say yes to my right to live and my right to be safe and healthy. If you are like I was and have low self-esteem and self-worth, saying yes to yourself can be the hardest thing to do. Know that you can and will do it. It may take several tries and saying yes in very small ways at first, but you will do it when you are fully ready.

In which ways do you say YES to yourself and your life? Was there ever a time when you had trouble saying yes?

Reflection

Yes

Goals

1.

2.

3.

Zest

"True happiness comes from the joy of deeds well done, the zest of creating things new." Antoine de Saint-Exupery

Zest involves enthusiasm and passion. It turns its nose up to apathy. I think we all enjoy those times where we feel such excitement and energy about something.

I have lived much of my life feeling a zest for learning and knowledge, as well as travel. What I have only recently learned is how to have a real zest for life itself. I have to attribute this change to my daughter. I used to be so goal-oriented that living life took a backseat. Now, I get to see this little human wake up every morning with a shine in her eyes just excited for a new day. Her days (and some nights unfortunately) are full of zest. The sun and moon amaze her. The wind's effect on the trees amazes her. The sound of a train in the distance intrigues her. The idea of "next time" and "tomorrow" fill her with anticipation.

As the last entry in this book, I want you to spend most of your time focused on zest in your own life rather than reading more about mine.

What are you passionate about? What energizes you? Do you live life with zest? If so, in which ways? If not, why not? What needs to change for you to be able to live a life full of zest?

Reflection

Zest

Goals

1.

2.

3.

Printed in the United States
By Bookmasters